One-Pot Camp Cooking
Quick. Easy. Delicious.

by

Pati and Carson Miller

This is not a traditional cookbook. It is a book about the craft of outdoor travel cooking. It is not just pages of recipes stuffed between two sheets of glossy cardboard like the world's most tasteless sandwich. Yes, we will share many of our favorite mealtime concoctions. More importantly, we will show you how to plan meals, choose ingredients, and minimize the fuss so you can spend more time exploring – with a full and happy tummy.

Disclaimer

We share the information in this book for your use and entertainment, but you must assume personal responsibility if you attempt to use any of the techniques and recipes found within. If you are not willing to accept that responsibility you should just put the book down right now. If you don't have prior experience with safe cooking hygiene and working around open flames you should go learn those skills first. If you are allergic to an ingredient we suggest, you probably should make a substitution. If you dump scalding hot water down your frontside, or backside, that's on you. If you give yourself food poisoning by heating up that week-old fish that seems "ok" you'll have to deal with the consequences. And if you invite a bear into your campsite… well, again, that's on you.

Be smart. Be safe. Eat well. Have fun.

Ok. Still with us? Let's carry on.

Acknowledgments

We would both like to acknowledge the moral and financial support of our parents, Carson and Barbara Miller, and Tom and Cheryl Rose. They never blinked an eye when we first shared our crazy idea of driving to Alaska and back, camping along the way. And when gas prices skyrocketed, they chipped in to help offset the fuel expense and make the trip viable.

Also, a big shout-out across the pond to Dave Sanderson. Dave is an internationally published ex-photographer, wannabe ex-waiter, and Instagram friend. He provided the motivation for this project when he jumped into self-publishing and showed that it could be done by mere mortals.

And a special thank you to our proofreader, Carrigan Miller. No amount of editing was going to make this a great book, but through her effort, it is definitely a better book than it would have been.

How It All Started

I looked up from the book I was reading, "I think we should go to Alaska."

My husband glanced up from whatever he was doing on the laptop, "Uh. Okay. Do you mean like fly up? Or take a cruise?"

"No, like camping. Like the overland travel people on YouTube."

"Uh." Long pause. "Okay."

That's how the trip of a lifetime started.

It's not like we were new to camping. We have a rooftop tent that lives full-time on top of our 2016 Jeep Wrangler. We've camped in the Everglades of southern Florida, the temperate rain forests of the Olympic Peninsula, along the sandy shore of the Gulf of Mexico, and deep in the forests of the Cascades. But never for more than a few days at a time. And we were never more than a few hours from the nearest Walmart.

Inspired by the overland adventures of YouTube explorers like Dan Grec of The Road Chose Me, Eva Zubek, Expedition Overland, and Lifestyle Overland we began to plan our own epic road trip from Central Florida to Alaska and back. A journey that would take seven weeks and cover over 14,000 miles. As we worked through the logistics of such an extended trip one challenge that kept popping up was food.

Like most people, we enjoy eating tasty things. But when you are planning a road trip through some of the most remote areas in North America there are a few challenges:

- We would rather be spending our time exploring than cooking or washing dishes.
- Eating at restaurants can be expensive and time-consuming.
- We don't like doing dishes.
- We don't have a ton of space to carry bulky food items, and grocery stores can be few and far between.
- We really, really don't like doing dishes!

This inspired us to explore the culinary "art" of one-pot cooking. Making delicious meals, using a simple set of ingredients, with minimal cleanup required. In this book, we share what we have learned so that you too can get maximum enjoyment, and minimal fuss when cooking on the move.

The Authors at the Alaska border.

Crafting Your Meal

Most of our one-pot meals follow a simple formula:

A base + protein + seasoning + anything else you have laying around you want to add

The goal is to assemble all of these things into a tasty dish using only one pot. After all, nobody likes doing dishes. Occasionally you may run into someone who proclaims they love doing dishes, but such claims seem dubious.

It's all about the base…

The base of most of our meals is typically a grain or starch. Couscous is a delicious and easy-to-prepare starting point for many of our recipes. We like the Near East brand Wild Mushroom & Herb and the Roasted Garlic & Olive Oil varieties best but feel free to experiment with different brands and flavors.

One advantage to couscous is easy preparation. Mix the spice pack into the pot of water and bring to a boil. Then add in the couscous, cover, and wait five minutes. That's it! You now have a base for your meal. The couscous requires about 1 ¼ cups of water. You can also add olive oil or butter, but we typically leave these out to reduce the number of ingredients we have to bring along.

Rice makes another quick and easy base for meals. We like the packages of "Ben's Original Ready Rice" and the Vigo brand of pre-seasoned rice. These are easy to pack, travel well, and make a tasty starting point for many recipes. Just dump the rice in the pot and follow the instructions. In a few minutes, you are ready to go! Spanish Style and Roasted Chicken are two of our favorite flavors. They are very versatile and can be used in a variety of dishes.

Mashed potatoes are another great option to get your creation off to a good start. Pouches of instant mashed potatoes are a quick and delicious starter to a meal. Boil two cups of water, stir in the potatoes, and you have your base. We like to have "Idahoan Butter & Herb" in our dry goods box.

All of these are good options because they take up minimal space, are inexpensive, are easy to find at the grocery, have long shelf lives, do not require any special storage, and are quick and easy to prepare. If your travels will take you across international borders, we strongly recommend that you keep these ingredients in their original packaging. Countries can have very specific rules about what types of food you can, and cannot, bring across the border. For example, at the time of our travels rice could be brought into Canada, but only from specific countries of origin. If your rice was in the original packaging it was quick and easy for the officers to inspect it and let you go about your travels. If you took the same rice and put it in an unmarked container it could, at the discretion of the officer, be confiscated. It may be tempting to consolidate your goods to save space, but if you will be crossing a border it is probably not worth it.

Protein, please...

Some grains like quinoa and brown rice, among others, have a decent amount of protein. Although not necessary for every meal, we like to add additional protein to most of our dishes.

A variety of meats are available in shelf-stable packaging that does not require refrigeration. Canned chunked chicken is one of our favorites. It is pre-cooked so you can simply add it to your base, warm it up, and enjoy. Dried meats are another fun option. We enjoy picking up cured dry sausage and meats for a little local flavor. And don't forget about the magic of leftovers. When we would stop and eat at restaurants any leftovers would go into the cooler to make a repeat appearance in the next day's dinner.

There are plenty of vegan and vegetarian protein options as well. Black beans and red beans are two of our favorite additions. You can buy dry beans, but it can take a long time soaking to prepare them for use. We typically use canned beans for convenience and easy storage.

Spice it up...

A bowl of rice and beans is a perfectly satisfactory meal, but almost everything tastes better with a little seasoning. However, this is a very personal choice so you will need to decide what works best for you. To keep things light we selected a few go-to spices that can be used in a variety of dishes.

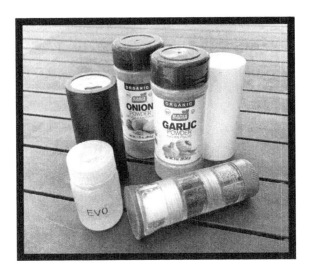

These are the spices we took on our journey:
- Salt
- Pepper
- Chicken Fajita Seasoning (Fiesta Brand from San Antonio, Texas is our favorite!)
- Garlic powder
- Onion powder
- Cajun seasoning, aka *"Bayou Blast"*

You can make your own *"Bayou Blast"* from Emeril's recipe:
- 2 1/2 tablespoons paprika
- 2 tablespoons salt
- 2 tablespoons garlic powder
- 1 tablespoon black pepper
- 1 tablespoon onion powder
- 1 tablespoon cayenne pepper
- 1 tablespoon dried oregano
- 1 tablespoon dried thyme

Mix ingredients thoroughly, store in an airtight container.

Super Sauces

In addition to traditional spices, there are a few other goodies you may want to have on hand. We have fun recipes that benefit from a jar of gravy or a splash of Worcestershire Sauce.

We try to keep the variations to a minimum, but here are the items that made the cut:
- Brown gravy
- Pizza sauce
- Cholula hot sauce

Cheese It

Cheese has become a staple of the American diet. We like to put that stuff on everything. Most of the recipes you will find here stand well on their own and don't call for cheese, but if cheese is your thing feel free to load it up. Stash some of your favorite varieties in the cooler and use them as you see fit. We like to use goat cheese - Chavrie Original is a favorite. It comes in a pyramid-shaped container. It is soft and melts easily. We also use the traditional three-cheese-blend shredded cheese as a topping for a little extra flavor.

Now Go Do It!

The key to creating your own delicious concoction is to think about the things you like best, pick a few, and experiment with different ingredients and variations. With just a handful of ingredients, you can make almost endless combinations. We had fun experimenting for several months before our expedition to dial in our recipes and perfect the techniques. Better to do it at home where a pizza is only a phone call away rather than wait until you are out in the wilderness. So why wait – next time you go to the store pick up a few things and give it a go!

In the following chapters we will share additional insights on choosing your fire and cooking gear, cooking and clean-up tips, and general camping cooking safety and etiquette. If you are ready to see our one-pot recipes and no-pot deserts you can skip ahead to page 31.

Carson enjoying a bowl of Chicken Tortilla soup.

Choose Your Fire

It's important to think about how you are going to cook your meals before you head out into the wild. You have several choices, each with unique pros and cons.

Campfire

There is nothing quite as romantic, or smokey, as cooking over an open fire. It conjures up images of cowboys circled around a roaring campfire while dinner simmers in a giant cast iron Dutch Oven. Cooking over an open fire can be fun and delicious, but it comes with several challenges.

Starting a campfire can be a tricky task. Weather conditions may not be on your side. We have been in situations where starting a fire was nearly impossible. Rain. Wet wood. Wet ground. Soggy everything. Other times strong winds made the fire hard to light, and harder to control.

Once you get a good fire started, it takes time to get it burned down to the point where you have a nice bed of coals to cook with. Then you have to let it die down and make sure it is completely out before you can go to bed or move on.

Wood for your campfire can also be problematic. To prevent spreading harmful insects many areas have made it illegal to transport firewood, so you can't bring it from home, or even your previous campsite. This means you will have to purchase firewood at each stop or scavenge for it where permitted. At the time of this publication, many of the National and Provincial Parks in Canada provide free firewood. Some will even deliver it to your campsite.

Local burn bans can also spoil your plans. In our travels, we have visited many areas where open flames of any type were not allowed due to the threat of wildfires.

We love a good campfire and some of our favorite meals have been cooked over a bed of hot coals, but for all of the above reasons we don't recommend it as a primary cooking method. If you decide cooking over an open fire is the way to go, we strongly recommend having a backup cooking method.

Charcoal

Charcoal is a good alternative to wood fires. You don't have to worry about transporting, buying, or rounding up wood. You may also have fewer burn ban restrictions, although some areas will restrict all open flames.

Charcoal is easy to use and can be ready quickly, although you will still have to make sure it is put out properly after you are done.

On the downside, charcoal is heavy and bulky to transport. It can also be very messy. You will want to have a small grill or cooking grate for those camp locations that don't provide one. In our experience, charcoal is a great solution for a few days of car camping, but not a great option for extended trips. Like using wood fires, it is probably a good idea to have alternatives.

Gas Stoves

We found a gas camp stove to be the best solution for our style of camping. These stoves can utilize a variety of fuels – propane, kerosene, white gas, and even gasoline. They typically come in one or two-burner configurations. Our go-to for our trip to Alaska was an old two-burner Coleman propane stove. It has been serving us reliably on trips for over thirty years.

The stove sets up quickly and uses one-pound propane bottles that can be purchased just about anywhere. It is very efficient. On our seven-week Alaska trip, we only used two propane cylinders. You can start cooking immediately, and when you are done it cools down fast and can be cleaned up and put away quickly.

Because it is not considered an open flame this type of stove can be used in areas that have burn bans. They can also safely be used in cooking shelters and under awnings in foul weather, and don't generate smoke or soot. However, you should never use a camp stove inside a tent or other enclosed space.

We also use a tiny single-burner backpacking stove for those times when we just want to quickly boil some water without the hassle of setting up the Coleman. This tiny stove screws onto the top of a small butane canister and is the perfect solution when you just want water for a hot cup of coffee in the morning.

Ultimately the best choice for you will depend on how and where you plan to camp, what you plan to cook, and how much space you have for gear. Whatever you choose for your primary cooking source, we do recommend that you have a backup option. Even if you are committed to the open-fire lifestyle there will be times when for any number of reasons, you just want a quick, hot meal before crawling in bed!

Campfire Tales – Fire Failure

We enjoy a nice campfire when we have the opportunity. Many Canadian Provincial Parks provide free firewood and dedicated fire rings. A few will even deliver firewood to your site, so there is no excuse not to light up – if you can.

I like to think I'm pretty good at starting fires. I have years of practice from teaching Boy Scouts and countless camping trips. I even managed to get a good fire going in the temperate rainforests of the Olympic Peninsula in the middle of a rainstorm. But it was our first visit to the Canadian Rockies where I met my match.

One rule of the Provincial Parks in Canada is that if a fire ring is provided, you have to use it if you make a fire. You can't just go off building a fire anywhere you want. One of our first campsites in Canada provided what looked like a very nice fire ring. It ultimately turned out to be a pit of frustration and despair!

The fire ring was much narrower than any I had seen before – it looked like they had taken a piece of 18" steel pipe out of one of the local mining operations, cut off a two-foot section, welded a steel grate on the top, and buried the whole thing about a foot and half in the ground. (Talking with some locals I believe this is exactly what happened.)

If you talk to a Boy Scout, they should be able to tell you that you need three things to successfully build a fire: fuel, heat, and oxygen. We had a good source of fuel – an almost endless supply of pine that should burn hot and fast. But whoever designed the fire pit had clearly not considered the other two ingredients. The pit was deep and narrow, making it difficult to draw in air. It also had a small lake at the bottom from accumulated rainwater. This was going to be a challenge!

It's hard to light a fire underwater, so the first step was to bail out as much of the standing water as possible. At first, it felt like I was trying to empty a well, as it seemed that the water just kept filling in the hole. But eventually, I was able to get down to a semi-solid bed of somewhat squishy, water-logged, ash. A few pieces of wood on the bottom provided a dry base to build the fire.

Getting the fire to take at the bottom of this hole proved an even greater challenge. After a few false starts and a face full of smoke I "cheated" and resorted to using a fire starter. These tiny logs of wax and wood chips normally will get any fire going in short order. I danced around the pit, fanning the fire with the lid from one of our storage boxes, muttering words of encouragement and frustration. No doubt any onlooker would have thought I was conducting some sort of ancient ritual – perhaps a sacrifice to the gods of smoke.

Occasionally the fire would provide a brief tease by sprouting a few tentative flames. But each time, as soon as I stopped fanning and feeding it a steady flow of air it would return to billowing a thick cloud of grey smoke. After several attempts I surrendered, having already sacrificed at least three fire starters to the campfire gods. I plopped down in a camp chair and watched the smoke slowly fade. Defeated. When I resigned to my fate and looked around, I could see thick clouds of smoke arising from other campsites in the distance. I couldn't see directly, but in my mind, I imagined other fellow campers dancing around their bottomless smoke holes uttering their own incantations with naïve hopes of nice, warm campfires.

The fire pit of despair.

Your Camping Kitchen

Not surprisingly, the most important item in your one-pot camping kitchen is going to be your pot. What is the best pot? Honestly, whatever pot you have will probably work just fine. You will want one that is just big enough, without being too big. The more people you have to feed, the bigger the pot you will need.

Weight can also be a consideration. A giant cast iron cauldron is probably not a good choice unless you plan on cooking all of your meals over an open campfire. But you also don't have to shell out top dollar for an ultralight titanium pot unless you also plan to use it for remote backpacking.

For our trip, we used a two-liter anodized aluminum non-stick pot made by Primus, because that is what we happened to have in our existing camp gear. Whatever you have in your kitchen will likely be just fine.

In addition to a pot, you may want to include a small kettle for those times when you just want to heat water for tea or a cup of coffee. Sure, you could use a pot for this purpose, but a kettle is arguably easier and safer.

To round out your kitchen you will want plates/bowls, utensils, and something to hold your favorite beverages. Again, whatever you already have will likely serve you well. We prefer bowls over plates, but either will work. Our bowls are made of stainless steel, which makes them easy to clean – but they get very hot to the touch. (We have "bowl koozies" to make it comfortable to hold the hot bowls. Think pot holder, shaped to cradle a bowl.)

Plastic may be just as easy to clean but can melt around a fire. On rare occasions, we even use paper bowls when we are just making a quick stop. A fistful of spoons and forks from your kitchen will work fine, or you may want to pick up the backpacker's favorite – a plastic spork.

For drinks, we have a pair of stainless-steel insulated cups. They are perfect for keeping hot drinks hot and cold drinks cold.

Our assortment of kitchen gear.

A few other items you will probably want:

- sharp kitchen knife
- small plastic scraper to scrape off any leftover food (makes the dishwashing process that much easier)
- long-handled wooden spoon
- pot holder or oven mitt
- can opener

So, there you have it. Go raid your kitchen. Grab a good pot, a few bowls or plates, and a fist full of silverware and you are ready to begin your adventure.

Our cooking setup.

Cooking in the Wild Outdoors

You have probably experienced cooking out at local parks or other locations that provide a nice grill and picnic table, but that is not always the case. Some of the best campsites are primitive sites in remote locations that may have no amenities at all. These situations require some special considerations.

Be Bear Aware

Will you be camping in an area where there are bears? Probably. Bears can be found throughout most of North America. It is always a good idea to act as though you are in bear country. If you are in an area of known bear activity you should take special precautions.

The primary rule is never to leave food, or anything that smells, out where a bear can get to it. This includes non-food items like toothpaste and deodorant.

If you are in a developed campground in bear country the campground will likely provide "bear lockers" for storing your smellables. As long as you have a hard-sided vehicle you can keep these items in your vehicle – just make sure you leave the windows closed. Also make sure that any trash is placed in bear-proof trash bins, or safely stowed in your vehicle.

If you are camping in a tent, never store or consume food in your tent. You don't want a curious bear interrupting your beauty sleep.

Level and Dry

You will want your camp kitchen to be as level and dry as possible. Fighting to keep your pot from sliding off the stove while cowering in a cold drizzle is never fun. Many Provincial campgrounds in Canada provide covered communal cooking shelters. These typically have a wood stove or fire pit and several picnic tables. They are a great way to get out of the elements and meet fellow campers. It also allows you to prepare all the critter-tempting, tasty treats safely away from your campsite.

Of course, you will not have this luxury if you are wild camping. In these situations, you may want a small, portable table for a workspace and a tarp or awning for protection from wet weather. A 10x10-foot tarp and some cord is a cheap insurance policy against a rainy spell.

We installed a fold-down tray on the tailgate of our Jeep that can be used for food prep and a place to set up our Coleman stove. Our meals were almost always prepared using this "tailgate kitchen."

Water

A final consideration is drinking water. Many of the locations we camped at in Canada and Alaska did not have potable drinking water. If they had water at all, it often required boiling or purification. You will want to make sure you have enough good drinking water for several days.

How much water you will need will depend on the number of people, the climate, and how you are using the water. We found that in the cooler weather in the north we used about a gallon per person per day for drinking, food preparation, and basic hygiene. Individual results will vary.

The best container for storing water? As with most other things, the best is likely whatever you already have. We have two, 2.5-gallon, plastic containers intended for water storage. You could just as easily repurpose gallon milk jugs or any other container that is food safe. That old rusty jerry can you found behind your uncle's shed? Maybe not.

Campfire Tails – Snack Attack

We were participating in a Jeep trail ride in the Sierra Nevadas and had arrived at base camp high in the mountains. This was an established camp so the local Black Bears were familiar with it and were frequent visitors. Our guides all carried "bear horns" on their belts to help deter the visitors if needed.

We slept in canvas tents – the type you might have seen in old war films, or possibly have slept in if you are a very old Boy Scout. Our guides were very specific – don't take anything into your tent that has a scent. This included not only food and snacks but deodorant, toothpaste, and literally anything that has a smell. All of our "smellables" were collected by the guides and placed in a large metal box that was hoisted up between two trees, supposedly safe from the furry marauders.

Bears have evolved very fine sniffers and apparently can smell these human things from miles away. And since this was an established camp, the bears were always close by. You could almost feel them watching from the shadows of the tree line, salivating over their next potential snack.

Each tent had a pair of cots and that was pretty much it. I spread my bedroll out on the cot and placed my pack at the foot of the bed – right up against the thin sheet of canvas that separated me from the bears. I figured, if a bear wanted anything in my pack there was no sense in making it hard on them. Perhaps the pack would provide a distraction while I escaped. As I lay in my cot considering sleep, I kept having one thought over and over – "Why don't I get a bear horn?"

I'm not sure what time it was when the chaos erupted, but it was pitch black outside. The blasts of bear horns rousted us from our bed rolls. Outside the tent, you could hear our guides running around. In between horn blasts, the guides shouted, "Stay in your tents! Do not come out of your tents!" Ripping, grinding sounds. More horns. More shouts – "Go away bear! Go away bear!" Then quiet.

The guides came around to each tent to tell us "Everything is ok. Everything is fine. You can go back to sleep." I don't know about the others, but there was no more sleep for me that night. Sunrise seemed forever away.

In the morning we could get a clear view of the mayhem that had taken place. Our Jeeps did not have tops, and a Black Bear had crawled into one and proceeded to dismantle the dashboard in an attempt to get to a granola bar that was stashed in the glove box. The Jeep was totaled – wires were strewn everywhere. Only the remains of a shiny wrapper hinted at the motivation for the carnage.

The guide asked the driver why he had left the granola bar in the glovebox despite all of the warnings, the driver responded, "It was all sealed up. I didn't think the bears would be able to smell it!" The guide replied, "That stuff is like bear candy! They can smell it right through the wrapper."

Lesson learned. Play it safe. Use "bear boxes" when available. Keep food and anything "smellable" inside your secured vehicle. And never eat or keep food in your tent – the only smelly thing in your tent should be you! – Carson Miller

Carson posing with one of the Jeeps that survived the "Snack Attack"

Clean Up

Have we mentioned that we don't like cleaning dishes? One of the many advantages of the one-pot cooking style is it minimizes the effort when it is time to clean up.

Here is our general dishwashing process:

The first, and most important, step is to be a "clean plater!" You don't have to eat everything on your plate, but you should make sure that the plate or bowl is scraped clean of as much food as possible before you wash it. This makes the actual washing process faster, more effective, and arguably less icky.

Using a plastic scraper, remove any leftover food residue from your cook pot and any dishes. Anything you scrape out should be properly disposed of – don't toss it around your camp or you will be certain to attract visitors. The goal is to get the dishes as clean as possible before actually washing them.

Fill your cook pot about halfway with clean water and bring to a near boil. Add a few drops of biodegradable dish soap to the hot water. This soap can be purchased online or anywhere camping gear is sold. A small bottle will be enough to last for weeks of camping. You don't need to bring the water to a full boil, but you will want it to be very hot.

Dip each item in the hot, soapy water and use a brush or wash rag to remove any food residue. We prefer using a brush so we don't have to deal with damp, smelly wash rags.

Set the clean items aside to drip dry, or hand them to your travel partner to hand dry.

Give the cooking pot a good scrub, then let the water cool before discarding. If you did a good job scraping your plates the water in the pot should still be in pretty decent shape. If it looks all nasty like some sort of gross stew you probably need to work on getting the dishes scraped cleaner. When the water is cool strain out any food bits and dispose of them in the trash. Take the leftover water at least 200 feet away from your camp before pouring it out on the ground. Do not dump it out near any streams, ponds, or other water sources.

Developed campgrounds may provide a central dishwashing station for your use. Be prepared to provide your own soap. Also, be prepared to wait in line at busy campgrounds. Take comfort in knowing you will look like a camping master standing in line with your one pot while the camper in front of you slogs through their assortment of pots, pans, plates, cups, and silverware.

Scrub-a-Dub-Dub – One-Pot Dish Washing

Many Provincial Parks, State Parks, and commercial parks will have dedicated dishwashing stations. At these camps, we still follow the same dishwashing process, but we will take our pot of wash water and dump it at the wash station and give our pot a good rinse.

At times you can get a pretty good line at the wash station. This is a great opportunity to chat with your fellow campers while you wait your turn. At one of the Canadian National Parks, I was waiting for the camper in front of me to wash a full laundry basket of dishes. It was a heaping basket full of bowls, dishes, cups, pots, pans, and assorted utensils. It appeared they were doing dishes for an entire platoon.

I stood there patiently with my one pot and a little scrubby brush watching the mountain tops turn orange in the last of the day's light. It occurred to me that perhaps I should have brought a headlamp. After a few minutes, the exasperated dish scrubber saw me – "Is that all you have!?" I looked around to make sure the comment was intended for me. "Um, yes," I replied, no doubt with a tone that sounded like I had been caught with my hand in the cookie jar. My fellow camper let out a deep sigh, "Please, go ahead. I'm going to be a while." I said thank you, stepped up and emptied my pot down the drain, gave it a ceremonial scrub followed by a quick rinse, and thanked them again before wishing them a good night and heading back to camp.

My new dish buddy gave me a puzzled look - I wasn't sure if it was admiration or disgust – then jumped back into the task at hand. The banging and clanging of pots and dishes faded in the distance as I made my way back to camp, dishes done for another day!
- Carson Miller

Our Favorite One-Pot Recipes

Here are some of our favorite recipes from the road. There is nothing precise or scientific about them. Think of them as suggestions. A starting point for your own creations and concoctions. Experiment with local ingredients. Make them your own. Have fun. Enjoy!

Note: Unlike other "cookbooks" you won't find any precise measurements here. No "half tablespoon" of this, or "3.5 ounces of that." It's camp cooking, not a chemistry lab. Most of these recipes are very forgiving, but when in doubt go easy on the seasoning to start. You can always juice it up later. Also, these recipes were made for two people. If you have more campers or are extra hungry, just double the recipe.

Pati enjoying Two-Can Soup.

Fiesta Couscous

We lived in San Antonio, Texas for over 16 years so we can't go too long without a little Tex-Mex flavor. Like all of our recipes, feel free to modify them to make them your own based on what you like, what you are willing to carry, or what you are lucky enough to find!

Ingredients:
- Couscous – Roasted Garlic and Olive Oil
- Precooked chicken, one can
- Black or refried beans, one can
- Chicken fajita seasoning
- ½ cup of shredded. cheese or one block of goat cheese

Preparation:
1. Add seasoning to water.
2. Bring water to a boil.
3. Turn off the heat and add couscous.
4. Cover and allow to set for 5 minutes.
5. Add chicken, beans, fajita seasoning, and anything else you want to dump in there.
6. Put back on heat, stirring occasionally until hot. (If using goat cheese this is a good time to add it.)
7. Serve – top with cheese if desired.

Chicken Tortilla Soup

Soups are always great on those cool evenings, or when feeling under the weather. This recipe will warm your belly and put a smile on your face.

Ingredients:
- Chicken broth, one box
- Precooked chicken, one can
- Black beans, one can
- Chicken fajita seasoning

Preparation:
1. Pour broth into pot and heat.
2. Stir in chicken and beans.
3. Add seasoning to taste.

Serve with a sprinkle of cheese and garnish with a tortilla chip if you have any!

Red Beans and Rice

This recipe makes a pretty decent version of the New Orleans classic!

Ingredients:

- Vigo Red Beans and Rice (You can use Ben's Ready Rice for an even quicker meal.)
- Andouille pre-cooked sausage (Any pre-cooked smoked sausage will also work.)
- Pre-cooked chicken, one can (optional)

Preparation:

1. Bring water to a boil.
2. Add red beans and rice and cook for 22 – 25 minutes.
3. Add sliced sausage.
4. Drain and add chicken (optional.)
5. Continue heating until meat is hot through the center.
6. Serve hot!

Kielbasa & Potato Foil Packets

This simple recipe can be cooked in a pot or skillet, but it is fun and easy to cook in aluminum foil packets over a campfire or stove – no cleanup needed. Kielbasa is a widely available Polish sausage that normally comes pre-cooked, so all you have to do is warm it up. Andouille sausage can be a fun substitute if you want a more Cajun spin.

Ingredients:
- Kielbasa pre-cooked sausage
- Baby potatoes (or any waxy potato)
- Onion
- Spices (Salt and onion powder will do the trick. Try some Bayou Blast if you want a more Creole flavor.)
- Heavy-duty aluminum foil

Preparation:
1. Cut the sausage into thin slices.
2. Cut the potato into chunks no larger than 1"x1" so they don't take forever to cook.
3. Coarsely chop the onion, trying to keep the layers together – thin slivers tend to get too crunchy.
4. Place the ingredients in the center of a large piece of heavy-duty aluminum foil. (You can add a layer of parchment paper if you don't want to cook directly on the aluminum foil.)
5. Add seasoning.
6. Fold the edges of the aluminum foil to make a secure packet. (See How to Make a Foil Packet below.) If you are cooking for several people you may want to make

one packet for every one or two people rather than trying to stuff all the ingredients into one packet.

7. Place on the grill, grate, or directly on a bed of coals.
8. Cook for ten minutes, then flip and cook for another eight to ten minutes.
9. Remove from the heat and allow to cool.

Bonus points if you shape the foil into a bowl and eat directly out of it!

How to Make a Foil Packet

Fold the foil lengthwise over the food and crimp the long edge.

Fold each end toward the center to seal the packet.

Classic Camp Chili Mac

You could just take a can of chili and a box of macaroni and cheese and dump them in a pot, but this recipe elevates the dorm room staple to a level worthy of the great outdoors.

Ingredients:
- Chunky chili with beans, one can
- Petite diced tomatoes, one can, do not drain (For a spicier version, substitute a can of Rotel.)
- Beef broth, one can
- Mild chili seasoning mix, one pack
- Uncooked elbow macaroni or small shells, two cups
- Velveeta cheese, diced, 4 ounces
- Shredded cheese of your choice

Preparation:
1. Over medium-high heat, stir together the canned chili, petite diced tomatoes, beef broth, and chili seasoning.
2. Bring water to a boil, stirring frequently.
3. Reduce heat to medium-low and stir in the uncooked macaroni.
4. Cover pot with lid and let simmer for 10 – 14 minutes, stirring every few minutes to prevent burning.
5. Stir in the Velveeta cheese and one cup of the shredded cheese until it is melted and has become one with the chili.
6. Remove from heat, top with the remaining shredded cheese, cover and let set for two minutes.
7. Serve hot! Pairs well with Fritos!

Two-Can Veggie Soup

This one is as simple as it gets. Open two cans and heat. It is also a good recipe for using up any leftover meat or fresh veggies from a previous meal.

Ingredients:
- Broth of your choice, one can
- Mixed vegetables, one can
- Last night's leftovers

Preparation:
1. Add broth and veggies to your pot.
2. If you have any fresh veggies feel free to chop them up and add them.
3. Any meat left over from yesterday can also make a savory addition.
4. Stir while heating.
5. Serve hot.

Yellow Rice and Chicken

This recipe is a recreation of the Spanish classic, ready in less than 30 minutes.

Ingredients:
* Vigo Yellow Rice, pre-seasoned
* Pre-cooked chicken, one can
* Diced red peppers (optional)
* Peas (optional)

Preparation:
1. Bring water to a boil.
2. Add yellow rice and cook for 22 – 25 minutes.
3. Drain chicken and stir in.
4. Add any additional vegetables.
5. Cook for a few additional minutes until the meat is hot in the center.
6. Serve hot!

Pizza In a Pot

Pizza is a favorite, but difficult to pull off on the road. This simple dish has all the flavor and none of the fuss.

Ingredients:
- Couscous – Wild Mushroom and Herb
- Pizza sauce, small jar
- Mini pepperoni, bag
- Mushrooms, small can
- Cheese

* Anything else you like to add to your pizza!

Preparation:
1. Add seasoning to water.
2. Bring water to a boil.
3. Turn off the heat and add couscous.
4. Cover and allow to set for 5 minutes.
5. Put back on the heat.
6. Stir in pizza sauce.
7. Add pepperoni and other "toppings"
8. Dish out and top with a sprinkle of cheese.

Campfire Cajun

No matter where the road takes you, you can always take a taste of the bayou with you. This is one of our favorite couscous meals. We prefer Emeril's Essence Creole Seasoning, aka Bayou Blast, but any Cajun seasoning should work just fine!

Ingredients:
- Couscous – Roasted Garlic and Olive Oil
- Andouille sausage, precooked
- Pre-cooked chicken, one can
- Tiny shrimp, small can (optional)
- Tomato sauce, small can
- Cajun seasoning

Preparation:
1. Cut sausage into small chunks.
2. Add seasoning to water.
3. Bring water to a boil.
4. Turn off the heat and add couscous.
5. Cover and allow to set for 5 minutes.
6. Put back on the heat.
7. Stir in tomato sauce.
8. Add chicken, sausage, and shrimp.
9. Add Cajun seasoning to taste.

Campfire Nachos

Whether for a snack or a meal, nachos are always a favorite. These nachos can be made from a variety of fresh and/or canned ingredients. The possibilities are limited only by your imagination, and what you happen to have on hand.

Ingredients:
- Tortilla chips
- Cheese (Shredded Mexican is a favorite.)

Optional Ingredients:
- Browned ground beef or chicken (You can prepare this in your pot beforehand.)
- Peppers (Jalapeños and roasted chiles are a favorite.)
- Black beans
- Fire roasted tomatoes
- Black olives
- Fresh items like onions and avocado make great additions

Preparation:
1. The secret to great nachos is in the layers. One layer of chips, followed by one layer of cheese and toppings.
2. Repeat until you run out of chips or room in your pot, keeping enough cheese and toppings for a final top layer.
3. Cover the top of the pot with a lid or layer of heavy-duty aluminum foil. This will trap the steam inside to help melt the cheese and soften the tortilla chips. Place the pot over heat until the cheese is melted.

Classic Beans and Weenies

No camping cookbook would be complete without Beans and Weenies. This backwoods favorite is as simple as it gets!

Ingredients:
- Baked beans, one can
- Hotdogs
- Brown sugar
- Worcestershire sauce (optional)
- Ketchup and mustard (optional)

Preparation:
1. Heat beans in your pot. One can of beans is perfect for two people. For a larger group just add another can for each two additional people.
2. Cut the hot dogs into slices about one-half inch thick. As a rule of thumb, we usually include one hot dog per person, plus "one for the pot." You can adjust based on how hungry your crew is!
3. Stir in the brown sugar, making sure it gets mixed in thoroughly.
4. Stir in the hot dog slices and heat until the slices are hot in the center.
5. For additional flavor, consider stirring in a little ketchup and mustard.
6. And for just a little more zing, add a dash of Worcestershire sauce.

No-Pot Treats

The only thing better than minimal dishes to wash is no dishes to wash! The following are some of our favorite camp desserts and other treats that don't require any dishes at all. Most of the recipes were originally intended for cooking over a campfire but can be adapted for cooking over a gas grill.

Many of these recipes traditionally call for added sugar and salt. We have omitted these ingredients from most of our versions. Fewer ingredients to carry, and arguably healthier. The one exception is brown sugar. Some of these just don't work without brown sugar, so it earns a place in our dry goods box.

All cooking times are approximate. Very approximate. Cooking temperatures over open fires can vary greatly. When possible, it is best to cook over a bed of coals for nice, even cooking. Cooking directly in or over large flames is a good way to burn your food.

Be very careful when using metal "forks" for cooking. They will stay extremely hot for several minutes after being removed from the fire. A good rule of thumb around campfires – assume everything is hot and act accordingly!

For recipes that require aluminum foil, we recommend the heavy-duty variety as it is less likely to tear or burn through. If you don't like cooking directly on aluminum foil, you can add a layer of parchment paper between your food and the foil.

Grilled Strawberry Shortcake Skewers

This is a great treat when you stumble upon fresh fruit during your travels. The recipe also works well with pineapple, peaches, nectarines, rhubarb, and pears. No fresh fruit? Canned fruit makes a good substitute. Canned pineapple chunks work really well. For a decadent touch, you can top it off with some whipped cream! (We recommend the kind that comes in the aerosol can so that in an emergency you can just shoot it straight into your mouth.)

Ingredients:
- Fruit of your choice, cut into large chunks
- Small, store-bought shortcakes
- Whipped cream
- Skewers
- Heavy-duty aluminum foil

Preparation:
1. Cut the fruit into large chunks.
2. Cut the shortcake into chunks. (Save any leftovers for breakfast tomorrow!)
3. Place the fruit and cake chunks onto the skewers.
4. If you have a grill over your campfire, lay the skewers directly on it. If not, you can wrap the skewers in aluminum foil and lay the foil onto the coals.
5. It will only take a few minutes to warm the fruit and release the flavors.
6. Remove the skewers from the fire and place the fruit and shortbread into a bowl.
7. Top with a generous shot of whipped cream.

Campfire Baked Apples

Another summer camp favorite, best suited for cooking over an open fire.

Ingredients:
- Apples
- Rolled oats (Granola will also work just fine.)
- Brown sugar
- Butter (optional)
- Cinnamon (optional)
- Whipped cream (optional)
- Heavy-duty aluminum foil

Preparation:
1. Let your fire burn down to a bed of hot coals.
2. Mix the filling ingredients (oats, brown sugar, butter, and cinnamon.)
3. Using a spoon, carve out the center of each apple. Be sure to remove the core, plus a little extra. The more room in there, the more room for the filling. But don't carve through the bottom or your filling will run out of the hole and you will be sad.
4. Fill each apple with the filling mixture.
5. Wrap each apple in a double layer of aluminum foil.
6. Using tongs, burry each apple in a bed of coals and allow it to cook for approximately 20 minutes. When fully cooked the apples should be soft, the filling crunchy on top and soft in the middle.
7. Carefully remove the apples from the fire and remove the foil.
8. Place in a bowl and load up with whipped cream!

Grilled Peach Crisp

Like apples, peaches are great for campfire grilling. If you can score some fresh peaches, this makes a fun and tasty treat.

Ingredients:
- Whole peaches
- Granola
- Brown sugar
- Butter (optional)
- Whipped cream (optional)
- Heavy-duty aluminum foil

Preparation:
1. Cut the whole peaches in half and remove the pits. Coat each half with brown sugar (butter optional.)
2. Place each peach half, cut side down, on a sheet of aluminum foil and crimp the edges to make a small packet around the peach.
3. Place the packets on a grill grate for approximately 15 minutes. You can remove the packets to check progress at any time.
4. Remove the packets from the grill and allow them to rest for a few minutes.
5. Carefully open each packet and use a spoon or fork to flip the peach halves over. They should be tender with a coating of caramelized sugar.
6. Top each serving with a spoonful of granola, and a shot of whipped cream if desired.

Tin Foil Monkey Bread

Anyone that has been to summer camp has had the campfire staple of Monkey Bread.

Ingredients:
- Biscuits, 1 can
- Butter
- Brown sugar
- Sugar (optional)
- Cinnamon (optional)
- Heavy-duty aluminum foil

Preparation:
1. Spray two aluminum foil sheets with nonstick cooking spray and set aside.
2. Mix sugar and cinnamon together (optional)
3. Cut each biscuit into four pieces and roll in the cinnamon mixture.
4. Divide biscuit pieces between the two foil packets.
5. Cut butter into small cubes and split evenly between the two servings.
6. Sprinkle with brown sugar and seal packets tightly by folding up the edges
7. Cook on a grate over hot coals for about 20 minutes or until biscuits are cooked through, turning frequently for even cooking.

Funky Chunky Chocolate Chip Cookies

This super simple recipe takes the ease of ready-bake cookies and levels up the flavor! When travelling we often find interesting local chocolate bars. Pick up a few and give this treat a try.

Ingredients:
* Ready-bake chocolate chip cookie dough
* One or more chocolate bars of flavors of your choice (Or a small package of M&Ms for color!)
* Heavy-duty aluminum foil

Preparation:
1. Line your pot with parchment paper or a double layer of aluminum foil. (A cast iron skillet will also work well if you have one.)
2. Spread the ready-bake cookie dough evenly across the bottom of the pot.
3. Cut or break your chocolate bars into large chunks and spread them evenly across the cookie dough.
4. Cover the pot with a lid or layer of aluminum foil to keep the heat in.
5. Cook on the lowest heat possible. If using a campfire, use indirect heat to avoid scorching.
6. The cookie is ready when the edges start to brown and the middle starts to set.
7. Remove the pot from the heat and allow to cool.
8. Using the parchment paper or aluminum foil, carefully lift the cookie out of the pot.

Fire-Cooked Eggs (In Shell)

A fun, easy treat for egg lovers. Young ones especially enjoy this cooking magic trick!

Ingredients:
- Eggs
- Something to poke a hole in your eggs

Preparation:
1. Poke a hole in the smaller end of each egg to allow the steam to escape.
2. Gently place the eggs directly on fresh coals.
3. Allow the eggs to cook for 5 – 6 minutes. Shorter if you prefer soft-boiled, longer if you prefer hard-boiled.
4. Carefully remove the eggs and allow them to cool.
5. Peel your egg and enjoy.
6. Add salt to taste if you desire.

Wrap Up

We hope you have enjoyed our little how-to guide for one-pot camp cooking. Hopefully, you have been inspired to give one-pot cooking a try on your next adventure. Pick a recipe, tweak it to make it your own, and give it a go. Instead of doing a bunch of dishes, use that time to roast a marshmallow, look at the stars, or tell a campfire story. Most of all, enjoy the experience!

If you liked this book, we hope you will tell your friends about it. If for some reason it wasn't your thing, consider gifting it to a friend that might enjoy it. After all, a book lives to be read!

Happy travels! Happy camping! Happy cooking!

All it takes is a pot. And maybe a kettle.

About the Authors

Pati and Carson Miller left the traditional workforce in 2019, choosing a road less traveled. They bought a motorcoach and started a lifestyle of working as little as necessary and traveling as much as possible. Since setting out on the road they have visited 36 states, including Alaska. They have driven both coastal highways from end-to-end, and have driven as far as one can drive in the continental US to the south, west, and east.

In 2022 they completed an epic road trip from Central Florida to Alaska, and back. For this adventure, they left the RV behind and camped along much of the 14,000 miles in a roof-top tent pitched on the top of their Jeep Wrangler. The lessons learned on this expedition regarding how to eat well, with minimum mess, and with few dishes were the inspiration for the book One-Pot Camp Cooking.

Pati and Carson Miller at the start of the Alaska Highway – 2022
www.wanderingdillos.com

Printed in Great Britain
by Amazon